One and, a Telling

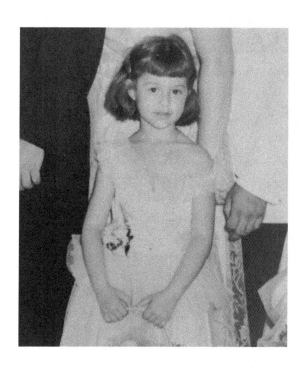

Poems by Eve Rifkah

Luchador Press

Big Tuna, TX

Copyright ©Eve Rifkah, 2021

First Edition: 1 3 5 7 9 10 8 6 4 2

ISBN: 978-1-952411-81-6

LCCN: 2021949783

Cover art: Eve Rifkah

Author photo: Betty Jenewin.

Acknowledgments:

"Buttons" / poetryfoundation.org/poetrymagazine,

"Wishes," "Runaway," "Almonds," "Hunger" / Segue@muohio.
   edu & Segue 5th anniversary issue,

"Dolls" / *Under the Roc,*

"Gift" / *Four Corners,*

"Straws," "Museum," "School" / SNReview.org,

"Path" / poetrysz.blogspot.com,

"Escape," "Picnic" / *The Worcester Review,*

"Tiger," "Mr. T," / *The Academy of Heart and Mind,*

"Garden" / *The Visitant,*

"Narcissus" / *The Pangolin Review,*

"Color," "Night," "Green," "Story," "Canton" / *Noh Place
   Anthology*

"House", "Change" / *Stone Quarterly*

Special thanks to Susan Roney-O'Brien, Jennifer Freed,
John Hodgen and the Rosemont Group

Dedicated to the Codman Square Branch Library
and the children's librarians Diane Farrell and Dorothy
Carrico-Wood. Wherever they may be.

The title comes from a song that ends the Passover Seder. It is a parable of the history of the Jewish people. A telling is the translation of Haggadah, the book that contains the Seder service. The poems are a telling of my childhood.

TABLE OF CONTENTS

For Colin,
Michael

In certain ways writing is a form of prayer
-Denise Levertov

Runaway

The kid reaches for knob
tries to open door of attic
apartment   all tight spaces

The dad asks   where are you going?
The kid wants away   wants gone
wants outa here   the kid
knows trap   knows steel-teeth clench
      knows fear on inside.

The kid tells the dad, wants going
the dad opens door
dark stairs drop down and down
the dad walks with the kid   stair
by stair   at bottom
   opens last door
        cold air races in
streetlights through tree branches
shake shadows like fingers like claws.
The dad asks   where will you go?
The kid looks out to dark
to impossible
no way to go alone.
turns back to door
climbs stairs.

Almonds

The ma used Jergens.
Narrow-necked bottle bibbed
in a black label   scent of almonds   of poison.

The kid breathed in   tainted
each in   hale
each breath-blackening sigh.

The kid took to breathing into a fuzzy lamb
centered on a blanket   dragged every-
where   breathed hollow   breathed deep.

The ma cuts bits
each day blanket shrinks
to lost lamb   then   to gone.

The kid turns to breathing blanket
bindings   silken borders ragged
and rent   pajama sleeves
patterns fade inexplicably   a gray
persisting   the kid cuts cuff from sleeve.
Hides it for years.

Wedding

The ma and the kid go downtown.
The kid needs a dress to be
a flower girl   a favorite aunt
to marry.   Jordan's   Filene's
up escalators   down escalators
nothin right   at home
ma pissed says   no way
not you down that aisle.

Nana calls   bought dress all blue net
scratchy and stiff'
The kid knows bout making do
bout not being right   bout the eyes
telling the kid is wrong.

The kid scared down the aisle
with fat cross-eyed cousin
dressed in pink satin
not room nuf for kid on skinny carpet.
Flowers in basket stay put
can't throw   just hold
in two hands basket center front.
Dress straps slide off shoulders
grandma angry
at ma who can't sew a few
stitches   to fix   what's wrong
with that woman, the grandma says.

Embellishment

Strange man comes to door
top floor three decker
brings out books
Colliers black and red encyclopedia
the dad touches a book
listens to salesman.

The dad buys the twenty books
enough to fill two shelves
in nearly empty bookcase
with bonus ten volume
The New Junior Classics
each book a different color
illustrations the kid loves.

Each night the dad reads
volume one fairy tales and fables
volume two stories of myth and magic.
by volume three the kid reads
page by page book by book
over and over, Pegasus
Thor, inhales new words -
embellishment the kid keeps
stashed away to sound out in dark times
em bell ish ment   the kid likes the sound.

Buttons

So what – pissed off kid spits out.
Sew buttons – the ma replies.
Like that means something
    like not getting an answer
        like it just don't matter what the kid thinks
on account of the kid is a kid
and the ma she just don't have an answer for nuthin
  and never did   cepting she's the ma.

You know how it is.

Or maybe you don't, maybe
your ma had answers
like on television
in houses where furniture don't scratch
and linoleum don't crack

But the kid knows it's all cracked
where the kid lives
and the ma knows it too.

Buttons hold clothes closed
    like not open
    like keeping inside
    like not letting on.
Buttons keeps clothes together
    not like home, nothing together there

more like not naked
which don't mean not torn
        or faded or even that they fit.
Safety pins hold skirts tight
to not fall down
cause the ma don't sew
well, much of anything though she
does have needles
and a coupla spools of thread

What for? The kid again.
To sew. The ma again.
What? Buttons?

Tornado

Go out and play the ma said.
The kid looks up and down empty street
sitting on front steps
play what the kid wonders
no one here
the kid lonely
looks up through tree leaf to sky
funny how sky is yellow
never was yellow before
blues and grays and night black
sometimes stars but not many in city
streetlight   store light   traffic light
on this day yellow.
and wind   trees bend
leaves swirl.   Things up there
flying
sticks   papers   things unknown.

The kid goes back inside up many stairs
tells the ma about yellow sky
the ma looks out
doesn't say anything
until the dad comes home
tells of tornado in Worcester
homes destroyed
something strange, dad says,
this not being tornado country.

Said couches and beds falling
from sky into bay.
The kid doesn't know Worcester
where's that the kid asks.

Narcissus

The ma buys bulbs and tiny stones
in pale colors
places stones in bowl
set bulbs into stones
and water.

Narcissus, the ma said
flowers
bowl on little table
next to window
for light
the kid can see from bed.

Every day the kid watches
green shoots grow taller
until little buds appear
open into white flowers
scenting the room
like something wild
something wonderful.

Color

The dad's thick fingers smudged
he concentrates   holding tiny
bit of ochre   one hand   sienna other
a TV table holds a box of pastels.

The kid gazes at blue paper
a lady's soft eyes stare back
her hand holds a folded fan.

The kid's fingers itch for color
wants being an artist too.
asks for pastels to use.
The dad says   don't touch.

The dad angry when the kid gets
gifts of kits of paint-by-number
thinks aunts should know better
buy real thing.
Why won't the dad?
the kid wonders.

The ma turns magazine pages
in next room
eating nonpareils.

4 rooms

The kid thinks this room a nightmare
glares at red brick wall
across gravel driveway
day dark as storm.

The ma angry too
wants better   white stove not black
not old-fashioned
hot water without match-lit burner
wait for heat up
wants better
wants real house
picture window
like her sisters who married better.

In pantry a single bulb
all dark and scuttle
where sink is
shelves with cans, canisters
pots and pans.

The kid wonders why move here
from big apartment top floor
all sun and space
the kid knows it's nice the dad
doesn't have to shovel coal in a cellar
here turn a dial and heat comes

here market around the corner
drug store next door
bus stop close by
the kid doesn't miss scary landlady
but wants light, wants looking out window
to see sky.

Dolls

Ginny sits all day
dressed in plaid
in crocheted hat and shawl
nowhere to go.

Ginny, says kid, know how it is.
The kid moves arms and legs
Ginny stands   Ginny sits.
don't much matter, says the kid.

Look out that door   and there's
another   out there and stuck.
The kid says   even with real legs
nowhere to go.

Only so far
            and turn 'round
or sit on curb grow cold
look at houses   can't go in.

All doors locked
the kid says   other mas pick up phone
call the ma
the ma be pissed cause she gotta move

off that couch with her crochet hook
and knitting needles   only things
the ma knows to do.

Ginny don't answer.

Never does, don't matter.
The kid knows a doll is a doll
no talking no nuthin'
no different from a shoe.

S'posed to be happy with dolls
but don't nobody askin' what the kid wants.
dolls crowding with their hard arms
all those empty eyes.

Night

The kid lies in bed wanting to turn on light
not wanting to see
scurrying things   scurrying things
move so fast.

They are there   over the edge
between here and need.
The kid holds on tight
wants to make it through
to other side of night.

Clenches eyes   wills feeling to go away
clicks on light
tiptoes   not wanting to touch floor
sticky floor   rattle and scuttle
floor where dark things live
in bathroom
held breath
and light
and
                        there
against white porcelain
in damp dark stains under faucet.

In morning another wet bed
the ma angry
screams.

Someday the kid thinks
someday enough years stuffed behind
and night will just be night.

Green

The kid sees   more green than
the kid ever thought possible
           beyond three-deckers, eyes everywhere.

The kid thinks Monet   like in museum
the kid goes with the dad
place the ma won't go.

The kid don't know arboretum
           not country

    climbs twisted tree
                    hides in leaves.

Down at bottom   the ma   the dad
dark inside leaf umbrella.

Now sun   blind   eyes close
body in shade
head stuck out on top
           tree a gown
like in fairy tales   goin' to ball
no prince kiss here
           no wand-ed ladies to tap
           and home begone.

The kid stays in green in sun in dark

till the dad calls.

The kid says   want to stay   want home in trees.

Hunger

The kid picks at scab of dried something
         on fork
looks down straw before lowering to glass.
Chocolate milk
                never white
never anything   like from the ma.

The kid forks mashed potatoes flat
searching out lumps to miss
         lumps to stick
to   block all air
to suff o cate.

Wishes the ma would
as the ma crams   white bread   chicken
fat   into her maw.

Mermaids

The kid stands on firm wet sand
left by outgoing tide
watches as the dad
sculpts a life-sized mermaid
hair flowing over one breast
fish tail curves a letter J.

The ma looks away
the kid entranced.

The dad performs this every time
they go to beach
at home the kid watches
as the dad works on paper with soft pastels
portraits with sunset backdrops
for grumbling patrons.

The dad's nudes hide in ragged portfolio
yet beach beckons
seducing with possibilities
dissolving with incoming tide.

Piano

At Passover finding hidden matzah,
the kid asks for a piano.
Grandmother screams
how dare you
ask for so much
all the kid wanted was a piano.
The kid thinks, doesn't have to be new
slinks out of sight.

At relatives' house in Chelsea
the kid plays upright player piano
as grandfather clock at the foot of the stairs
peals Big Ben refrain.
The dad teaches *Frere Jacques, Mary had a little lamb*
over and over the kid plays until
old ladies say stop.   Say enough.

One day old ladies say
we will send piano.
The ma and the dad make room
next to the one bookcase
in square entry hall.
On day marked on calendar
the kid and the ma wait
              wait some more
until the ma calls old ladies,
changed their minds they say

not a word   not a sorry

all the kid wanted was a piano
to make music
sounds to live in
when words aren't enough.

School

The kid looks at pictures in primer
Maple Street   white houses
green shutters   trees.

Who lives like that?   the kid asks
wishin   to be someplace
not apartment

gravel backyard where cars park
even dad's Pontiac with light
up Indian.

See Puff run
run run run.

Who talks like that?   the kid asks
like askin God
not 'spectin an answer.

Even the dad pissed bout Maple Street
in schools where kids don't live like that
not that it matters   much.

The dad pissed bout lots of stuff
but don't never do nothing bout it
like when the kid n the dad shop for a plant
for grandma   mother's day

the kid thinks one with pretty red flowers nice
but grandma   yelled   gave it back.
How the kid know grandma hates flowers?

Or time the kid picks out shiny gold rollin-
pin with ball-bearings.
Grandma waves her ole wooden pin in air
says she not needin any new pin
this one works fine.

The dad mumbles all the way home
kid knows the dad scared too.

History

In the history book the kid
reads about Columbus
how people thought earth flat.
The kid imagines water running over edge
like an immense waterfall all around
why aren't the oceans empty?
where does new water come from?
what is underneath?

The kid thinks who would have thought
flat?
At beach horizon meets the sky
curved
and that sun rising and falling.

The kid confused
knowing that sailors would know
earth ball-like and spinning
following stars
setting charts.

Now the kid has doubts
about times written in books
what is real and what not?
who wrote those books?
why tell stories untrue?

Neverland

As the Tinkerbell light dims and slow fades
       Peter implores
If you believe   shout I believe

Clap your hands.
The kid sits   hands still
knows kids clapping everywhere
can almost hear

but knows a light is a light
knows life and death don't depend
       on this kid.

Light gets brighter
       as the kid knows it would,
sees wires
holding Peter, Wendy, the boys.

The kid fist-wipes tears
       doesn't want to be seen
       crying for a flickering light
feels a something heavy midway throat and belly.

Whispers a wanting
       something more than belief
       something hard and real.

Name

The ma opens the front door
sticks out her head
screams
                    Evie
the sound ratchets down the street
up the street
radiating out from that mouth,
that door, 7 Capen Street
lasso winds out until
the kid captured turns

the name taffy-pulled out
to end in scream screech eeeeeeeeeee
a sound the kid hates
with hunched shoulders
returns
no other way
not like the pet bird
loose from cage
freedom to fly around the living room

one day someone opens door to porch
bird flies out
the kid knows the bird will get caught
by a something not kind
the kid knows freedom doesn't last.

Skates

The dad hands the kid the aunt's old skates
skates made like boys'   ugly

the kid wants girl skates   figure skates
with notched front   pretty
the kid wants to skate
dad wants to teach the kid to skate

gives in   buys girls' skates   figure skates
beautiful the kid thinks
wants to glide like skaters on TV

on ice   slippery
the kid holds tight   rail one side
the dad's hand other
learns
side-to-side glide push
it comes   this sense of moving through
cold air   breath advancing

at Max Ulin rink in Milton
where the kid and the dad go
bus to Ashmont
orange trolley to Mattapan,
red and cream bus to Milton
new rink open to sky

surrounded by marsh and beyond woods
sun warm

in warming house long wood benches
wood stove scents air
a man makes cotton candy
swirls of pink cloud the kid never saw before
cloud that dissolves to tiny drop
sweet in mouth

ice, air, skates, cotton candy
fire warmth
finally someplace good.

Story

On the seventh day he rested.
For how long, the kid asked,

reading story of how it all began.
It being everything,
earth, sea, wind, birds, man.
It being all tangles
all woes.

For how long? the kid asks again.
Why doesn't he or
maybe she or perhaps it -
what is this thing called god, anyway?
wake up, take notice.
Or did god turn away
try again some other place?

The kid is full of questions
no one wants to answer.

the kid shakes head
returns book to shelf
keeps hoping for
something to make sense
in this forsaken world.

Drawing

At school the kid is told
make drawing of home.
The kid draws apartment house
six apartments a double three-decker.

In front the kid draws a tree.
The dad says no tree there
don't matter says the kid
who likes trees better
then gravel drive between brick
store backs and house.

The kid thinks drawing doesn't have to be real
though the kid likes paintings
in museum of real
how the dad says look
at light in drop of water
bit of gold on knife handle
Chardin.   As real as real can get.

But the kid wants a tree
in front.   Leaves shading summer heat.
only real tree at end of block
the giant fir in front of friend's house.
friend that lives in single family
with aunt, uncle, brothers, parents.
How nice would that be
the kid thinks.

Path

The kid thought invisible
        on no man's land
        behind houses lining Capen St.
        through woods – not real woods
        scattering of thin trees and underbrush.
The kid thought journey
        path from one backyard
        behind others to dead end dirt road.
The kid walked this trail
        not sidewalk – not in sight of
        curtained windows
to friend's house
        the younger kid
        whose parents wonder why
        fourth grader plays with second
        wonders what's wrong with this kid.
But the kid likes little house
        on dead-end – beside overgrown field.
The kid dreams of living in a house
        no sounds of doors opening
        slamming shut   no sounds
        of footsteps upstairs down
        voices behind the walls.
The kid wants living things outside windows
        not brickwall back of market
        gravel driveway cuts
between cars crunch crunch outside the kid's window.
The kid wants air to breathe   enough space
        to live.

Gift

The kid
surrounded by grandparents
great uncle and aunt
who wears three dresses on top of each other,
aunts, uncles, two cousins
with presents too
even birthdays shared
with those born on the right
side of grandmother's heart.

The kid opens a tiny suitcase
with plastic handle   pictures of cow
over moon a dish running
away with a spoon both on skinny legs,
slides red records from a paper folder

>   *She'll be coming round the mountain*
>   *Oh Susannah*
>   *The Walloping Window Blind*

At supermarket the dad buys
            The Nutcracker Suite
            Flight of the Bumblebee
            Mendelssohn, Schubert
three out of twenty classical masterpieces
in maroon boxes.

Enough to know   there's more
knows there's music for dreaming
someplace far away
someplace where the kid can dance
feet hardly touching
floor.

Museum

The kid and the dad ride trolley to museum
red line green line jiggles and shakes
right to front door
with statue of Indian on a horse
rain splatters the Indian's chest.

Inside big doors   marble and gold
paintings everyway
even on ceiling
the kid always impressed.

The dad fast walks through
tapestry room all chills
walls of stone
the dad never lets the kid look.

The dad has own direction
round circle stairway
Monet's   haystacks
Cathedral at Rouen.
The dad talks light and time
changes what we see.
The kid thinks   yeah so does
rain and cloud
change to dark.

The dad always turns right
at top of stairs
into realism, impressionism.
The kid knows isms
and artists   on first name basis
Claude, Edouard, Pierre, Vincent.
The kid dawdles picture to picture
up long hall   farmyards, flowers,
moonlight and mountain.
The kid sneaks peeks down hall
where pretty lady dances
getting bigger with each step.
The dad tells the kid stories
about artists about
favorite model.
The kid thinks beautiful
The kid thinks love.

Carp

In dark Asian rooms
the kid and the dad walk
by big statues
spooky   thinks the kid.
The kid wants lookn at fancy robes
stitched pictures of dragons
and mountains   the dad not interested.
The dad and the kid climb to balcony
look down on goldfish in long pools.
Carp   the dad says   from Muddy River
out back.
The kid's seen gold and splotched fish
glide in murk
but the kid thinks
fancy museum don't catch backyard fish
the kid don't say nothing
never does.

Nightmare

In bed the kid looks between windows
where picture the dad drew
leans against wall.
Portrait of woman with closed fan in hand
the kid thinks   why here   why in this room.
The kid huddles in wool blanket
binding frayed from the kid's breath.

Each night the dad's cursive name
in corner of portrait
becomes brown cocoon   every night
the kid holds breath   as snake emerges
grows ever larger to fill room
wraps the kid in tightening coils.
The kid gasps tries to pull in air.

The kid wants out
away from room with no view
away from day as dark as storm
art that kills.

Castle

On hot muggy nights
tree leaves painted still
the dad packs family
in Pontiac with light-up Indian
the kid fond of Indians
tries to be one walking so quiet.

The dad drives to Castle Island
not really an island
at least not anymore
road through Southie
by beaches
ends at parking lot
where Sullivan's sells fried clams
the dad never buys.

They skirt star-shaped fort
trees growing from top
to monument to Donald McKay
who designed big ships   American Clippers
sails like clouds riding the sea.
The ma and the dad sit on monument step.

The kid climbs on high ledge
walks around and around
traces shapes of ships
with fingers dipping in and out
bas-relief, the the dad says.

They go to catch a breeze
watch planes take off from Logan.
Ugly freighters pushed by tugs
slug glide to harbor.
Later walk long way around
back to car.
The kid watches people line up
at Sullivan's known all over Boston.
Stomach growling the kid
gets into back seat
of the two-toned blue and cream Pontiac
the dad's first ever car.

Passover

One kid, one kid that father bought for two zuzim.
One kid, one kid.
A Passover parable

Now what the dad won't say
is how can a cat eat a goat.

The kid figures out
the dog, the stick, the fire

but right there at the beginning
that cat ate the baby goat.

Don't know a cat can do that,
the kid says to the dad.

The dad shrugs   just a song
doesn't have to

make sense.   Would help
if it did says the kid

who isn't a goat just
a child trying to figure

it all out.   Gets bout being
on the bottom   the kid knows

lots bout the bottom
what with crazy ma

and steel-eyed grandma
hateful.   The kid knows

water can drown   fire burn
don't know bout that Angel

of Death or the Holy One
blessed may he be.

The kid knows nothin bout that
being always on the bottom

the one that gets eaten
first.

Beach

Every summer family crams
into grandfather's dark blue Dodge,
grandfather, grandmother,
great aunt, the mother,
the father, the kid.

In the trunk, towels,
picnic basket, big
green thermos, cool
aluminum glasses.

Following in their own car
aunt, uncle that never talks,
cousin.

On the beach they spread blankets
mark out territory.
Grandfather covers himself
in baby oil mixed with iodine
gleefully praising his concoction for tan
while the kid sifts sand
through a sieve.

They parade to waves
elbows bent   sidle in short steps and hops
hands flap   splash and tingle.
Old ladies back into waves
rolling over shoulders

till lunch time. Grandmother
unpacks turkey sandwiches with mustard,
half sour pickles and fruit,
lemonade from dented jug.

After lunch dads and moms take cousins
across street to amusement park.
In octagon building cousins
ride carousel dark in shade
from sunblind outside.

They walk littered park –
play skeet-ball for prizes
get frozen custard
best there is
flavors painted on colored slats.

Back at beach they flop on blankets.
The kid dozes to the chatter of voices
the shurring of waves.

end of day   dizzy with sun
prickly with sand
they pile back into cars
heat rising in wavy lines.
Scented with sweat and sea
sit silent on long roll back.
At bedtime, windows open
to catch hint of breeze, the dad rubs on
Noxema to chill the kid's red skin.

Holidays

The kid and the dad and granddad
go to temple   the kid sly touches
fur on ladies.
Inside always same bench first row balcony
can see everything.   The kid likes it here
the stars criss-crossed on ceiling
out long windows   open
to Indian summer heat.

The kid reads silent in English
don't sound nice as Hebrew.
The kid likes best shofar part
waits for sounds   puffed-cheek Rabbi
     blows words   the kid knows
    words are music.

The kid thinks god stuff
don't make much sense
but still likes it here.

After service walk to apartment
where grandmother and aunts
are cooking   but not the ma.
Here the kid stays small
not a peep
      not like perfect cousins
the kid black sheep   baa

                    fleece in mouth
          all dark and wrong.

          After lunch the kid sneaks out
          cross street to zoo   hides in garden
          with locked tower.   Never mind deer
          antelope   musk ox.
          The dad and uncles search
          call the kid's name.
          the kid waits it out   till the kid thinks time.
          Thinks better sitting in sun
          in sun not black sheep   no baa.
          The kid don't much care gets yelled at
          always gets yelled at some time or nother.

Straws

Spat and gag
the kid splutters mouthful
          cross table.
The kid knows Dark
          knows crawling inside
      inside then out.
                              Insect
scurriescrosstable.

The ma pissed again
      wipes rag   cross milky puddle
leaves stick   leaves tack
blur of sweet tea.

Roach   the kid yells
in straw   in mouth
alive   kid knows
                        fear inside out
                        outside in.

The ma shrugs
pissed at mess
          the kid makes.

Garden

The dad plants a garden
in tiny yard in front
of six family
digs up dead rose and forsythia.

In school the kid
gets a box of seeds
to sell for PTA.
The kid don't know anyone with land
for growing   all stuck in apartments.

The dad buys four packs,
marigolds, portulaca,
zinnia, balsam.
The dad finds old bricks
makes a ring in center of garden
to fill with flowers
and all along front border
tomatoes, cukes, peppers
all fit into little yard.

The kid and the dad climb
down from front porch
onto a stump or by front stairs
over old wire fence
with rotten wood frame.

When fall comes, dad shows the kid
how to get seeds from dead flowers
for next year   no need to buy from school.

The kid and the dad eat
tomatoes like heaven
straight from the garden
all sun warm and sweet
the kid likes all this growing stuff
sniffs fingers tomato scented.

The ma doesn't make sauce
or do canning
makes the kid sell tomatoes
door to door
fifty cents a pound.

Tiger

In tiny variety store
girls show the kid   kittens
in back room.   Owner wants homes.

The kid tells the dad   want kitten
want holding soft alive
want something real to love.

At six weeks, the kid
carries tiny meow voice
pinprick claws home.
The kid names Tippy
the dad asks why that name
the kid shrugs   sounds like a cat name.

The dad gets a box   fills with dirt
shoveled from out back
bathroom dad says.
The ma mumbles about cleaning
about smell.

When kitten becomes cat
goes in an out
until the day
car going fast
cat crossing street
gone.

Mr. T

The kid tries again
at little store
another litter.

The kid picks black and white
tuxedo, store man said.
This one named Mr. Tuffy.

On TV a man teaches linoleum block printing.
The dad buys x-acto knives, linoleum
ink and roller.

The kid draws portrait of cat
with perfect heart on chest
the dad explains transfer
drawing to linoleum
everything cut away white
what remains black.

The kid makes cards
sends to family.

Mr. T settles in
until the day
out minding own cat business
when dog
all angry teeth
outa nowhere.

The kid retreats to lonely again
as the dad buries the dead.

Dance

At Chanukah grandpa said   Hebrew School
or dance lessons.
The kid didn't think too hard

chose ballet.
The dad opens encyclopedia
looks under B for ballet
a photo of Maria Tallchief
hands crossed over chest.
Beautiful   the kid thinks.

In the dad's art books
Degas' dancers
the kid takes out pencils and pad
draws dancers.

The ma and the kid take a bus
then a trolley to Mattapan
where dance teacher is
not a school just one room.
The kid amazed at the teacher's roundness
zaftig the kid's dad would say.
Not image the kid had in mind.

Dressed in leotard and
ballet shoes   the kid tries real hard
first position   second
plie   arabesque   glissard.

At recital time
the kid gets a skimpy lavender tutu
not like pictures seen in books.
The dad sprays black slippers
gold.

Dentist

Because the ma never takes the kid
to a dentist,
the kid goes with other poor kids
to state dentist
in basement under the library
in a big waiting room
kids fidget   chew on nails   whisper fears.

The kid is led to a room with machines
and tools spread out on paper.
In a big chair   the kid opens mouth
wide   so wide it hurts.

Dentist, a big man with big hands
goes into the kid's mouth
needles that hurt
then mouth numb and lips big rubbery.
Dentist drills into top of front teeth
cavities.
makes fillings to match to look invisible.

More fillings, silver in back teeth
one molar all black and hollow
pink gum shows through
dentist says leave alone
will fall out by itself.

Dentist asks if the kid sucks hard candy
the kid says, no doesn't like hard candy.
Dentist asks about lemons
yeah, lemons, likes to suck big yellow wincing slices.
Dentist says, don't do that
acid wears away enamel.

The kid goes back more times
the kid feels small in big chair
hates dentist who is doing his best.
The kid only wants own fingers in mouth
not stranger's   one finger crooked
from long time sucking middle fingers left hand.
What the kid does when all alone.

Picnic

The dad says
taking friends on a picnic
says they never get to woods
get away from city heat.
The ma says   what will neighbors think?
The dad says   his home is his home
don't matter what neighbors think.

Cause his friend is Negro
don't ever say nigger or even colored,
dad says to the kid.
Respect he says.
The kid knows names for others
cause the kid's family are Jews
which is like being not white
which is being different.

The dad's friend sweeps floor
where the dad works
friend even lower
than the dad   who never invited
anyone else from work.

They come in a big car   a
convertible car   friend and wife
and two little girls.

The kid scrunched between dad and ma
to picnic place
with Indian name   Chickatawbut.
In a lookout tower they see city
sunglint on windows
where the bay is
so blue.

Drive-in

The kid and parents go out
to drive-in movie.
Fancy neon sign shows way
to posts at every spot in big lot.
The dad fits big speaker
into window cranked up to hold.

The kid is wearing pajamas
a first time for going out
has blankets for just in case
though there's no sleep for this kid.

The ma gets popcorn and sodas
settles in.
On screen, monster squid
holds submarine
in tight grip.
The captain scared hacks
big arms with ax.
20,000 leagues
the kid don't know league
how deep. Too deep thinks the kid.

The kid sees tentacles and suckers
for nights on end
the kid always afraid now
of things before unknown.

Comfort

The kid wants to believe.
Looks at all others
in house of the lord.
The kid reads words
mouths words phonetically
Hebrew
reads translation
English.

The kid thinks all gobbledy-gook
wonders what is missing
wants something to depend on
knows talking to god
is no help.
Thinks of all words for god
allah   thor   zeus
knows some have been cast out.

The kid strokes cat.
Cat leans into the kid
pushing furry head into hand
a comfort the kid thinks
maybe all that is needed.

Wishes

I wish… said the kid.
If wishes were horses then beggars could ride
            the ma said again
and again.

The kid knows futile
learned early

no wish way out.
The kid stares at calendar
imagines piles of calendars to wade through
don't much matter what picture is
it's time that matters
all those days
all those years
till gone till outa here
away from crazy ma.

Wishes need waiting
need hoarding   need faith.

The kid doesn't know what to think of faith
but files away more wishes by every day

If wishes were love the kid would…
but the kid doesn't want to ride there.

Escape

The kid leaves house
at corner gets bus a nickel fare

The kid climbs stone stairs
pushes big oak doors
breathes in   out
sighs.

Surrounded in silence
until kid makes words speak
only to the kid.

Librarians put the kid to work
stamp stamp
dates on cards
more cards to file in little drawers
new cards on metal rod librarian
pulls out and cards settle in place.
The kid files away books from rolling
cart to shelves

lifting to tops of toes
stretches to reach high shelves
leaves books inch out.
Librarian checks make sure

the kid gets it right.   Here
sun melts on oak tables

here rain streaks trails on windows
here air smells good.

The kid breathes   deep
breathes good
breathes safe.

Friend

Her name came just before the kid's
first three letters same.
The kid loved friend's calico dresses
teeny flowers scattered on darkcolor
friend lived inside a garden.

Lived in a real house   a single family
two floors and an attic
with trunks of old clothes
like in stories the kid read.

The kid and friend dress in ball gowns
big high heels they trip about in
friend lived with a mom and a grandmom
no dad   the kid asked where's dad
no answer.

In winter grandmother makes a skating rink
in back yard from a kit   plastic liner
clipped to metal edge.
The kid and friend skate in tight circles
round and round
no straight out fast
no let loose   good just the same.

Afterwards grandmother serves cookies
and milk   the kid doesn't drink milk
nothing white.

The kid wants to live like this
in a real house   with a grandmother who bakes cookies
while mom works
an attic with beautiful clothes
a room with windows with view of trees and sky.

Twice the kid visits friend
is never asked again.

Difference

The girls learn to sew while boys
do something, the kid unsure about that part.

The kids in class are to get gingham
the kid doesn't hear part about
red.
In store picks out pink
and blue embroidery thread for initials.

In class all others have red
only the kid is pink
the kid don't care
What difference does it make?
A bag is a bag
will hold what is needed.

The kid learns stitches
basting, back stitch, blanket,
how to pull thread through bee's wax
so, it won't snarl
how to peddle the treadle machine
with the pretty designs
Singer.

In the last year the class is told to bring in cotton
but the kid doesn't hear part about white
and asks dad to buy blue

in class all others make white aprons
that cross over back
and a band that is sort of a hat
to keep hair away from food.
Across the bodice the kid
embroiders in pink thread
a name to match apron to owner.

Everyone will wear these aprons
in cooking class in a different school
in another year.

Brothers

After the sister lost
before birth
the ma had a son
born live.

The dad asks if the kid is jealous
the kid just shrugs
not much the kid can do.

Two years later another boy
ma doesn't want
cries for *a bor tion*.
Doc says no
says ma will love
what doc doesn't know….

Now five in four rooms.
The dad searches for a house
while babies cry.
The kid brings home books
and more books
hides away in stories
not the kid's own
somewhere else
to go while body stays still.

Pizza

The ma and the dad go out
a time alone
pizza and beer at neighborhood tavern.

The dad promises pizza
for babysitting little brother.
The kid loves pizza
from tavern

round and red
cheese that winds from mouth
back to crust

edges bubble
like a wave about to break
faint scent of yeast.

The kid stays in room
with a book propped
up on knees   stays real quiet

waits for pizza
in white flat box
waits for brief moment
of pleasure

Change

The kid knew aunts, uncles, cousins,
children of old Jews from Russia,
the Ukraine, Lithuania,
all moved to suburbs
all had fancy houses with picture windows
and lawns – big flat lawns
all around houses.

The kid learned word *exodus* at Passover
when the Jews up and left Egypt
with Moses, the head man.
The kid thinks Jews leaving Roxbury
an exodus of sorts.

They took their shul with them
or rather built a new one.
Old one with Jewish stars
across ceiling sold.
New owners splash acid
on stained-glass windows
color not their thing.
The kid thinks sad to live without color.

The dad says, people of color
are beautiful, are dressed in their skin
not naked like white people.
The kid thinks naked is naked
and skin is skin, all is fine.

On the streets round grandparents
people are dark now
are dressed in sienna, umber, burnt and raw,
cinnamon and a black so black
blue lights shine from their skin.

Grandparents move one last time.

Move

After brothers come
five bodies in four small rooms
and a square entry hall.

First brother moved to a cot
in hall
new one in crib
that was the kid's once upon a time

The dad searches for a house
not that the dad has money
cause the dad never has money
but grandad covers down payment
on VA loan.

The dad takes buses and trains and trolleys
turns away from new house
second floor unfinished
finds house from old times
house on main street of small town
bus stop in front.

buys the house grandad
advises against   the dad cries
wants this house.   though no one
knows why.

On a cold day in February
the dad and the kid go to clean
walk into cold house
pipes burst   no heat
the kid and the dad walk to only
store around   sells pizza and soft serve
dad uses phone   looks for help
the kid thinks bad start
to new life.

Back at the house
the dad makes fire in fireplace
what will be parents' room
uses old signs with painted numbers
and letters CD
dad says means civil defense
piled in back room
the paint blisters and peels
makes pretty blue flames
while they wait for fix-it man
to come and say how much.

The kid likes wide pine floors
with knotty hills and valleys
the kid's feet curve around
but not much else about place.
even though house is on original map of town
big deal, the kid thinks
it's now that counts
trying to live here
in not city not country
land.

House

In new but old house the kid
has a room in attic   a fireplace
the kid's not suppose to use
but does   secret flames
   the kid hunches over.

The kid's never seen walls so ugly
rain-stain brown stripes slant to strip of ceiling
the kid thinks army tent
cold ground   winter war
spring mud.

Straight walls dark olive drab
the kid thinks tanks and jeeps and uniforms.
On green, yellow roses float the size of cabbages
among scenes of New York   Statue of Liberty
Brooklyn Bridge   Tomb of the Unknown Soldier.
The kid thinks   who chose this?
Someone with hate
in their soul.
The kid's life wrapped in
hideous   like old fish   like trash.

The kid tries soak   tries scrape
knuckles rub raw   hours go by
only tiny space of wall shows through
the kid gives up   covers with pictures
cut from magazines.

The ma angry   the kid *des truc tive*
the ma says   Stop.   The kid don't care
wants away with yellow roses   liberty.

One window   north wall
never a slant of sun on pine floors
where knots stick up   curve into the kid's soles.
All furniture wobbles.
The kid dreams of oceans
taut sails aching.

Blood

The kid all comfy with book in bed
away from brothers   babies
stink of diapers
when the ma comes in with book
for the kid
says, remember when you asked
about the box in the bathroom?

Yeah, the kid says

The ma hands the kid pamphlet
How to Tell Your Daughter About Menstruation.
The kid thinks I'm not the ma
but rather read than listen to whatever ma has to say.
On the back page a list of books by Kotex
"Everything you need to know...."
can't even get right book, the kid thinks
reads anyway.

The ma returns ask, did you read?
Yeah, the kid answers.
What do you think?
The kid says, now I know how to tell
a daughter if I ever have one.

The kid knows about blood, about monthlies
some kids call the friend

though the kid doesn't understand
why blood and mess and pain
is a friend.
No one said there would be so much
pain and chills and the invisible
steel clamp that circles the kid's body.
No one said not every kid goes through this
much pain   chills that shudder the kid
blanket wrapped in front of raging fire
the dad made in fireplace in the parents' room.
The ma has nothing to say

Pet

You love cat more'n you love me   the ma yells.
The kid's new cat   shit on pillowcase
the ma angry   grabs knife
chases the kid round table.
The kid run fast
yells to friend   Help.
Friend thinks time to go home
never come back.

The kid   out door
down street
       into woods
knows the ma won't follow
cause the ma can't run   and don't care
now the kid is gone.

The kid curls up on big rock
quarry stone shaped like bed
shaded by thin tree
waits
the kid's real good at waiting
knows life-time of waiting.

Watches the sun   till way past noon
when the dad comes home
then walks slow walk
back.

Contest

At the old school the art teacher singles the kid out
for special assignment.
At home the kid's dad pulled a shade off lamp
on bureau, turned off other lights
gave kid white pencil
black paper
said draw light.

Art teacher sent home block of linoleum.
the kid has x-acto blades sent for
by the dad when the TV artist showed how
it was done.
Sometimes knife skips out
blood smears over white lines
on black.

Teacher enters the kid's portrait
into state contest

Art teacher takes the kid to ceremony
to see all other pictures
by kids in the state.
The kid twelve years old won blue ribbon
tiny gold key in square box.
The kid proud knows teacher proud too.

The dad doesn't leave work
see the kid get award.   Later on phone
the mean uncle tells of going
asks why wear ragged sweater
why no makeup?
Tells this to dad on phone
no words about award
nothing ever right for the kid
or the dad.

Suburbia

After move in mid-year
all cold and colder
the kid goes to new school
junior high   in new building
or seems new to this kid.

Everything different
the kid out of place.
In gym class the kid
wears dark blue bloomers
and white shirt from Boston
like the mom wore
back when.

The kid hates bloomers
old-fashioned in a bad way
in new school girls
wear one-piece outfits
with snaps down front
mint-green.

The kid wants to be special
asks teacher – home room
about making a mural
for St Pats day   pot of gold
leprechauns with striped tights.

Takes a long time to make
out of pieces of paper
drawn and cut and glued
not that other kids care
the kid wants hiding again
can't do anything right.

At home the kid finds it hard
to hide in room with no door
until the kid makes a curtain
with sewing machine bought
from Sears Roebuck catalogue
with the kid's own savings.

Canton

After big move to small town
the kid takes only town bus   one driver
goes home for lunch   6 pm last run.

At Mattapan rides free trolley
view of marshes   through a cemetery
free ride ends at Ashmont station
the kid takes red line to green line
to big library Copley Square.

The kid feels tiny
going up stone stairs between big lions
inside up more and more stairs
to little room with pictures
and tinier cramped room
with all the art books.

The kid reads van Gogh's letters
to brother Theo.
The kid lost in words so beautiful
thinks this man knew life
knew pain   the kid saw paintings
breathe   ones the kid didn't much like before.

The kid reverses trip
makes last bus home
a long way to go to read a book
a whole day out of the house
happy.

Grown

The kid now grown
wonders why continue
this litany of the past.
Wonders what is the point
of redoing what can't be redone.

It was what it was
as now is what it is
the grown kid looks out the window
the house across the street
empty for so long.

The kid feels empty too
all the years lost
in transit
all the changes
that never did feel quite right.

The kid still just a kid
no matter the years
that piled on like so many
calendars tossed away.

Chad Gadya / One Kid

One Kid, one kid that father bought for two zuzim. One Kid, one kid.

And the cat came and ate the kid that father bought for two zuzim. One Kid, one kid.

And the dog came and bit the cat that ate the kid that father bought for two zuzim. One Kid, one kid.

And the stick came and beat the dog that bit the cat that ate the kid that father bought for two zuzim. One kid, one kid.

And the fire came and burned the stick that beat the dog that bit the cat that ate the kid that father bought for two zuzim. One kid, one kid.

And the water came and quenched the fire that burned the stick that beat the dog that bit the cat that ate the kid that father bought for two zuzim. One kid, one kid.

And the ox came and drank the water that quenched the fire that burned the stick that beat the dog that bit the cat that ate the goat that father bought for two zuzim. One kid, one kid.

And the slaughter came and slaughtered the ox that drank the water that quenched the fire that burned the stick that beat the dog that bit the cat that ate the kid that father bought for two zuzim. One kid, one kid.

And the Angel of Death came and slew the slaughterer that slaughtered the ox that drank the water that quenched the fire that burned the stick that beat the dog that bit the cat that ate the goat that father bought for two zuzim. One kid, one kid.

And the Holy One, blessed is He, came and killed the Angel of Death that slew the slaughter that slaughtered the ox that drank the water that quenched the fire that burned the stick that beat the dog that bit the cat that ate the goat that father bought for two zuzim. One Kid, one kid.

Eve Rifkah was co-founder of Poetry Oasis, Inc. (1998-2012), a non-profit poetry association dedicated to education and promoting local poets. Founder, and editor of DINER, a literary magazine with a 7-year run. Presently she is a retired professor from Worcester Polytechnic Institute. She runs an ongoing writing workshop for 15 years and teaches workshops and classes at WISE (Worcester Institute for Senior Education). She lives in Worcester, MA with her husband, musician, artist, writer Michael Milligan and their cat.